M000191130

Love in a Suitcase

Relationship Notes from an
Analog Time for Our Digital World

Thomas Schwendler

Love in a Suitcase

For more information about this title or to order other books and/or electronic media, contact the publisher:

Publisher: Rev. Tom Schwendler
https://www.revtomschwendler.com/

ISBN:
978-1-7368130-2-7 (Hardcover)
978-1-7368130-0-3 (Paperback)
978-1-7368130-1-0 (eBook)

Printed in the United States of America

Cover and Interior design: Van-garde Imagery

A Thank You Note

Thanks to my wife and CFO on this project, Rosemary, for letting me use our 2021 Stimulus Check and more on this project. Grateful to fellow Marquette alums Kate and Sarah Klise for sharing their book expertise. And, thanks to our 'street team' - Kathy M, Matthew Y and others - for their feedback. Lastly, thanks to my aunt and uncle for sharing their love and wisdom.

Table of Contents

Foreword
(Actually, a look backward)

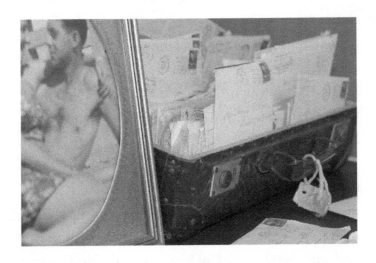

In 2020, a global pandemic exposed our interconnectedness and, in some cases, brought families and friends closer together. The virus drove us to be virtual with family gatherings taking place online, while face-to-face greetings were replaced by a phone call, text or email.

I became better connected to my aunt and uncle during this time even though they had been dead for more than a decade.

We reunited in my basement where I had retreated out of the boredom of self-isolation to take on the long procrastinated job of cleaning out the accumulation of clutter.

Lurking around the green ping-pong table, alongside a stack of books on a shelf outlining the perimeter of the basement floor, and ignoring the mounds of knick-knacks and pictures and cardboard boxes, I zeroed in on an old brown suitcase.

I knew it was there waiting for me since I snatched it from my uncle's apartment after he died in 2013. I knew there were love letters inside, and I didn't have the heart to trash them. I guess my uncle felt the same way as he had held onto these hundreds of letters for more than 60 years.

I had promised myself that I would read these letters someday. That day was now.

I opened the suitcase to reveal the hundreds of letters from the self-proclaimed "Small Town Boy" from Savannah, NY (Uncle Bill), and the "Big City Girl" about 130 miles away in Buffalo (Aunt Anne), spanning the start of their courtship in 1946 to their wedding in 1948.

I read them all—twice. While they had been separated into stacks—his and hers—most were not in chronological order. Still, I was able to piece together their journey and extract some nuggets of wisdom from a couple having an analog relationship that could be helpful advice in today's digital world. These are the same lessons I hoped to share with couples whose wedding I officiated but did not have the time to spare amid the haste of ceremony preparations.

I hope you'll enjoy what I've unpacked from this suitcase and maybe you'll learn a trick or two to nuture your relationships.

—Rev. Tom

Chapter 1
Communication Practices

When it comes to communicating, take the time to do it write!

If you write regularly, it takes the form of journaling—a common spiritual practice. Actions speak louder than words but let's start with the words for now.

Authenticity

Assuming you've got pretty good penmanship and your beloved doesn't end up cursing your cursive, there's no better way to communicate in an authentic and personal way than in a handwritten note.

There's some kind of alchemy going on when your thoughts move from your mind to your hands to a piece of paper. Because it's slower than a keystroke and takes more effort, your thoughts can be deeper than those expressed in a text message or a social media post.

Getting a real letter in the mail is a novelty these days. Let's face it, no matter how sweet a text message might be, no one is going to hold onto it for years. But, a letter can have an immediate and long-lasting impact. Getting a handwritten note can sometimes feel like you're getting a hug from the sender.

PS. Love you again, and you know, Bill is a lot more contented, works better and everything is better when he gets letters from you.
-Bill (Feb. 2, 1946)

Word choice

"Snip," "Punky," "Smooth," "Wim Wams," "Nerty"

Being a 'word' guy, I found these pronouns and adjectives to be quite amusing in these letters from the late 1940s. The point is that word choice matters and how you say it is just as important as what you say.

Ah, and what about those three little but really important words? Anne and Bill struggled too:

> *...About it being difficult for you to say you love me, I don't mind Bill but I will admit I don't understand. You see, Darling, to my way of thinking you would have to love me to account for your actions to me. Otherwise, maybe my baby is a bad boy. Regardless, I'm glad you don't use those 'Three Little Words" freely without feeling. I know when you do say 'I love you' you really mean it...*
>
> –Anne (Feb. 1948)

If you find yourself at a loss for words, then it must be time for a kiss.

Listen up!

The best communicators I've ever met are the best listeners. Did you hear what I said?

There's an adage in marketing that a brand must "Say it seven times" before a message sticks. While I think I'm a good listener, my wife can testify that she often has to tell me more than once about things . . . especially tasks I really don't want to do.

Transparency

Be a good Scout! Being upfront and honest builds trust. It's the opposite of being a "snow artist."

What's the good of having any secrets from one another. What's the good of having a girlfriend or boyfriend if they can't share each other's joys and sorrows. We've just got to be honest with one another. Please sweetheart...If you only knew how much I loved you and how much I think of our very nice times together, our happy future. Seems like paper just won't absorb my feelings for you. Nothing could – only I know how much I love you....

–Anne (April 1947)

Some levity

Don't know what to say or how to say it? Buy a greeting card.

Like handwritten letters, greeting cards are increasingly rare these days. I found a few holiday cards in the suitcase. Some can be pretty witty, but using your own words can show that you have a sense of humor. Being able to laugh is important to any relationship.

Try sharing a funny story or observation. I found this short note from Anne in a birthday card to Bill:

> *Bill-*
>
> *I never bought ties for a man before and I thought this would be a good time to get in a little practice. A male clerk helped me select them and when I told him that you were on the conservative side, he laughed and said that a tie*

is to a man what a hat is to a woman – 'a new lease on life' and when a woman bought a hat that went with nothing she owned – she just went out and bought something it did go with. Maybe you'll have to do the same.

– Anne

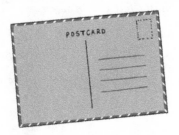

Some brevity

A short note is all you need to remind someone that you've been thinking about them, whether it's a text, a quick call or a sticky note left on the kitchen table.

You don't have to say a lot to mean a lot. Less can mean more. I found a few "ancient text messages" in the suitcase. These were short notes written on the back of bank deposit slips, checks, and yes, a one-cent postcard.

> *Working on my books and really shouldn't take time to write you but for some reason or another have an extra thought for you and wanted to say hello – Love you and wish you were here. Gee! I'm happy knowing that you love me and that you are contented, happy and know that I love you. Must close.*
>
> *– Bill*

If it's urgent

In the 'old days,' you might get a Western Union telegram with some important or urgent news like you've won the lottery. Telegrams were used to convey urgent and important news when you couldn't wait for US Mail Service or didn't have a phone.

If it's urgent, then text. But please not a lot. I have a "three texts" rule. Text me thrice about a topic, and I pick up the phone to terminate the texting tennis match. It's not that hard. Just pick up the phone! Clear the airwaves and enjoy the rest of your day.

Feedback and busy signals

How 'dialed in' do you feel with your partner? The only way you're going to know is to ask him/her.

"Checking for Understanding" is one of the cornerstones of a communications model developed by Guru Roger D'Aprix. Make sure you look for and get feedback when you communicate.

Stating your feelings and thoughts is important and sometimes he/she just won't get it. But, don't give up. Expect a few busy signals now and then. Just talk it out until you're sure that you are both on the same page (of paper).

Chapter 2
Conversations: 3 "Fs" – Finances, Faith, Family

Money matters, religion, and relatives may be among the most common and trying topics of conversations for couples. Here are some thoughts on the 3 "Fs"— Finances, Faith and Family.

Money matters

It's easy to get in over your head. Anne called it having "a steak appetite and a hot dog purse." Having a budget is one way to deal with money matters. So is having a healthy perspective. "A person can have a lot of money but nothing to show for it," said Anne. In other words, money isn't everything.

Shared goals

Weddings can cost a lot of money (*average of $30,000 in 2020*). But, that's something you can control. As a wedding officiant, I've joined couples for affordable ceremonies on the beach as well as the backyard. It's good to set a goal—together.

> *Been counting all our gold tonight and found that we have $1,400 cash and bonds,"* Bill wrote. *"That is, besides paying for the refrigerator and bottle cooler and our bills for this month. We only have $600 to go before we can get married. Know something? Bet we can almost make the grade about Sept. 15...*

Anne watched her spending, but she also counted their blessings.

> *You have a business and I've got a few dollars in the bank should we need some ready cash. And*

most of all Bill, we've got a certain feeling that is priceless...

My advice: invest in a marriage, not a wedding.

Little things count

"Watch your pennies, and the dollars will take care of themselves." That's some advice I got from my aunt, and she was right. Little things matter. Back then, long-distance phone calls required assistance from an operator who could either place a station-to-station call or a more expensive person-to-person. It was much cheaper to send a letter, as stamps cost three cents in the late 1940s. Anne and Bill also saved some money by having a wedding on a Saturday morning followed by a breakfast.

Religion commands attention

God gave Moses the Ten Commandments on two stone tablets. Maybe God is a letter writer too!

Marianne Williamson is another writer, internationally acclaimed author and lecturer on spirituality. In a 2012 interview with *Psychology Today*, she articulated a view that, in some ways, all relationships start with your relationship with God:

> *Real love has to do with a joining of the mind, a joining of the spirit, a joining of the heart. If we want the real thing, we have to create and cultivate a sacred space for it. Making the time, saying the prayers, doing the meditation, dealing with the issues in ourselves.*

Traditions

Anne and Bill lived out the belief that every relationship is a reflection of your relationship with God. Anne grew up Catholic and it played a big part of who she was. That was not so much the case with Bill although he had some spiritual leanings.

> ....*Just taking time before going to bed, to write. I wonder if you had a nice Christmas. Thought of you a lot over the weekend and Christmas. Oh! Last night went to midnight Mass. You know, just to see how me and the good Lord are making out. Still tells me He's running things – and the funny part of it – guess He is.*
>
> –Bill (December 25, 1945)

...I'll let you in on a little secret. I've been praying like this: 'Please God make Bill and I happy if we are supposed to get married. Please make it be the right thing; if not let it end in a nice way.' I guess it all amounts to this: 'Thy Will Be Done."

–Anne (March 1947)

Family ties

Today, when we talk about 'cutting the cord,' it's often about severing ties with cable TV. When it comes to relationships, it may be best to 'cut the cord' with our families.

In one of her letters, Anne etched out a simple line *drawing* on the back of an envelope. The idea behind the graphic was clearly to make the point that in a committed relationship, it's no longer ME/YOU. It's all about US.

We're so lucky so much more than most people and we're going to have something because it's us. Not you or I but us and we are trying now as well as later.

—Bill

It is going to be you and I first and if we have to cater a little, we will 'cause we'll be happier in the long run. You and I are going to be happy regardless of what anyone thinks, says or does.

—Anne

Blending back 'grounds'

It helps if you get along with your families. Meeting your future in-laws for the first time is as memorable as any "Kodak moment."

> *...I want to give you a full account of what my folks think of you. Mom said Anne doesn't eat very much. 'She did like the broccoli, didn't she?' She also said it's too bad Anne's mother couldn't have some of the broccoli (referring to some my brother brought home today.) I'll get more out of her tomorrow. I'm sure you must have created a good first impression as if you hadn't — Mom would have let me know before now. I do hope you like my folks. I won't ask you*

if you like Savannah. I would ask you if you could tolerate it…

And here is Anne's reflective response:

…So, your mom doesn't think I eat very much. I hope she didn't mind because I really was nervous and I couldn't eat. Gosh, Bill, I do want them to like me because I love you so very much.

You asked me to give you the truth about my visit to Savannah — Well, Darling, I guess I have. I like your folks very much because they think so much of my Bill. Just that short visit and I could see how much they think of you. As for the town, Darling, well, it isn't exactly Buffalo but I know wherever you are and where we could make a nice living is where I want to be. I really don't think you like the town Bill. Why?"

Chapter 3
Navigating the Relationship

It's not a linear progression, though traditionally we've expected relationships to advance from 'dating' to 'going steady' to 'engagement' to 'husband and wife.' That's what we think. But, as the old Yiddish proverb goes: "We plan, God laughs."

Sometimes you simply have let go and let God. At every stage of life, we make plans, setting out where we want to go and imagining what we will be like when we have "arrived." But things have a way of turning out not quite as we hoped or expected. Know that, along the way, there will be ups and downs, stops and starts as well as joys and disappointments. That's life as we know it.

Drivers and navigators

Long before cars came with navigation systems or any kind of GPS, we used to take along paper maps on our road trips. For those of us with AAA memberships, you could get a "TripTik," a collated booklet that literally traced your journey from start to finish with a colored marker.

The companion to a TripTik, which AAA still offers today, is a much larger and unwieldy state or local map that could be nicely folded and fit into the glove compartment. That is, if you had good dexterity and knew how to manage the folds and creases. Otherwise, it was a wrestling match. The point is that road trips were a two-person job with one person being the navigator and the other the driver. It's the same with relationships. Sometimes you're the driver and other times you're the navigator.

Long-distance relationships

Who'd a thought that a guy who lived on a muck farm in rural upstate New York could eventually marry a 'Big City Girl' from Buffalo, NY? Might seem like a bit of a stretch, given the distance. Maybe that was a good thing, says Jesuit theologian Henri Nouwen:

> *One of the mysteries of life is that memory can often bring us closer to each other more than can physical presence. The presence not only invites but also blocks communication.*

Anne and Bill were 130 miles apart but always only one thought away from each other. *"Maybe we gathered a few more memories because of the distance,"* Anne wrote.

Anticipation and alarms

You're in love and happy to be together. Things are really cooking. But, are you ready to take the next step, whatever that may be, in a relationship? Expect to have some doubts along the way. But eventually the doubt fades. It did for Anne by April 1948:

> *Know something Darling? I am really getting awfully excited about getting married. I'm losing all that scared feeling now. I just know that everything will be perfect with you as a husband. I need you Bill. I need that feeling of 'everything is alright' that you give me. I've never been too afraid of anything but just the word 'marriage' has always given me the thought that so very many marriages are failures and full of meanness, and how could I expect to have the*

exception. Just the other day, I read where sta-
tistics have proven that 3 out of every 5 mar-
riages have ended in divorce. It has gone higher
because of the war marriages, it said. Even with
reading that, I'm not afraid 'cause I know how
deeply I love you and just because you're you....

Ups and downs

In July of 1947, Anne had drafted a four-page letter to Bill, later tore it up and then wrote a short note. She sealed, stamped it and put it on the dining room table to mail on a Monday morning. She passed it a couple of times, thought about Bill, and all of a sudden picked it up and threw it in the garbage can.

> *Gosh, Bill, I don't know what has happened here. I do find it hard to sit down and write to you. Before, it was so easy. Never had to think a minute on what to say. I guess I did write just about every day. I hope I'm wrong Bill, but that 'living in the clouds' feeling seems to be gone…*

It happens. Don't worry about it.

Gee, life is a problem and when you stop to think Bill, life is for such a little while. Makes me think that we should be happy and satisfied regardless of how mixed up it seems to be at times...

Vows

You could see the change in Anne and Bill's relationship by the way they literally addressed each other in their letters. Over time, they went from "Dear" to "Darling" in their openings to "For Now" to "For Always" in their closings. Most manufacturers today offer "limited warranties," but if you want the lifetime guarantee in a relationship, then make sure to put it in the vows. We all know the marriage clause, "till death do us part."

Disagreements

Every relationship has an occasional wrinkle. We expect marriages to be partnerships. Like any 'deal,' there has to be an agreement. However, we should expect to have disagreements that almost always can be ironed out. It is best though to agree on some of the big topics like children and careers early on.

Anne seemed to have one deal-breaker. While she was ok with giving up her work at Chevy and supporting his business, which meant moving to a small town for some time, she raised a red flag when it came to living arrangements:

> *I won't plan on any wedding though 'till we have a place to live. Try to understand that one thing Bill... You know, sweet, if all I was thinking of was getting you as a husband, I could tell you all that confusion and what have you didn't bother me in the least, that I could like to*

live in the Ross home — just to get you and then after we are married turn the tables with a lot of arguing and fault finding with your family which would eventually lead to a feud. I believe in reasonably talking things over and trying to smooth things out before we get married.

Sharing a vision

Do you have a vision for your marriage? It's one of the questions on my questionnaire as I interview couples prior to writing a wedding ceremony. Anne did:

To me Bill, marriage isn't just a ceremony and getting a man to support you and to whom you act as a 'wife' in return for that support. To most girls, getting 'a man' is the most important thing in their lives. To me, the most important thing is getting a man who loves and cherishes me because of no particular reason — just because he loves me and he wouldn't trade me for Lana Turner even if she promised to shine his shoes every day of the week...

I want our relationship to be built on love, tenderness and consideration of one another. Being married to you, I'm sure of it. I've got that confidence in you Darling and that's why I love

you so. It's an awful lot Bill. Seems like there
is always something coming up that makes me
realize what a wonderful guy you are...

Patience

Long before digital cameras, all your photos were taken on a roll of film that had to be dropped off at a drug store or somewhere to be processed into prints. It sometimes took a week to get them back. Sometimes you just have to be patient with a relationship and see how it develops.

> *Never thought in a million years that I'd be sitting home writing to a guy 130 miles away on a Saturday night. Gosh, love is a funny thing but I'm glad it's you.*
>
> –Anne (Feb. 1947)

Chapter 4
Case Closed – Final Thoughts

The bulk of this book has highlighted the importance of communication. But, the bedrock of any long-term relationship is love and commitment.

Material is Immaterial

Focus on what's real and the joy of making something together. I can't say it any better than Anne did:

Gosh Bill, with his mansion of a home, his beautiful modern garage and showplace, his $3,100 car and all, I'll take my guy Bill. The only thing I did think was, 'why can't Bill and I have all this?' We will Bill and even though we don't get extra wealthy, we will accumulate something and with our love, we will have more than all that. A whole lot more. I couldn't see anything that I was envious of really. I guess it was 'cause I have you and if you didn't come with a deal like that I wouldn't want any part of it.

Being true

Listening to music in high fidelity meant having an audio experience that mirrors real life. In a relationship, we want to be heard and understood. In another sense of the word, we also want to be true to each other.

If your relationship leads to marriage, consider expressing your commitment to fidelity as part of your wedding vows. Here's a good example from one of the weddings where I was an officiant:

I, _____, take you, ____, as my companion in life.

To share our days in friendship and love.

To always be open and willing to listen.

To nurture and tend the Divine Light in you and in myself.

To give you the best of myself each day, as your loving and devoted _____,

For as long as we both shall live.

Be a collectible

Relationships will get scratched and damaged from wear and tear, but we don't throw them away. Let your relationship become a collectible. These two letters are real keepers:

July 1948

Dearest Bill,

Hello nice husband. It was a lot more than nice talking to you last nite. Can hardly wait 'till I see you tomorrow nite...Love only you for always. Glad you are my husband.

Your Wife,

Anne

⚹

July 15, 1948

To My New Employer,

Sorry to say I cannot accept position offered unless you can duplicate the attached (pay stub).

Very Truly Yours,

Anne Ross

PS. Don't take this too seriously. Maybe we can make a deal. Per my application, I'm easy to get along with.

Some Writing Assignments

In a way, all relationships are assignments. All our relationships are grounded first and foremost in our relationship with God. As assignments go, some are easy and others are hard. In keeping with the theme of this book—letters—here are some writing assignments to support your relationship.

Write an old-fashioned letter

While the typewriter may have gone the way of the corded phone, pens are still around, so use one. Don't waste time looking for fancy stationery. Anything will look fine. Bill even used bank deposit slips sometimes when he was on the run.

Write a letter to "My Future Self"

Explain why you committed yourself to this man or woman. That way, if you ever find yourself wondering, *'What was I thinking when I agreed to marry you?'* you'll know.

Write a prayer

Prayers are like letters to God. So, try writing one. Address it to "Creator" or to "Being" or whatever makes you the most comfortable if the word, "God," gets in the way. Then, find some quiet time and see if you hear the "voice" for God. You can be sure Someone is listening.

Send a card on National Mother-in-Law Day— the fourth Sunday in October

The day honors that special woman who brought the love of your life into this world. You'll score lots of points with this one.

Write your partner an IOU

Invoice your significant other. Free love may have been a thing in the 60s, but today, if you want love, it'll cost you. Here's what you owe: kisses, flowers, attention, etc. and an occasional love note.

Write some vows

Who says vows are just for weddings? Not me! I promise. Write a short note now—an expression of your commitment to each other. This is the old-fashioned "Lifetime Guarantee."

Write a dunning notice

What has he/she been late on? Arrange to settle a debt or work out a payment plan from the "lender of love."

Write me!

Tell me what you've learned about communication and share some of your tips from the "digital world." Email me at thomaschwendler@gmail.com

A Peek Inside the Suitcase

Mr. William A. Ross
Seneca Street
Savannah,

To The Nicest Husband in
The World:

First of all since
thanks again for a
wonderful honeymoon.

48

MARSHLAND
RESTAURANT
William A. Ross, Proprietor
SAVANNAH, N.Y.

Miss Anne M. Standish
46 Salem Ave
Buffalo
N.Y.

Anne darling —

BUFFALO
JAN 7
12 PM
1946
N. Y.

Mr. William A. Rew

Bill - I never bought ties for
a man before and I thought
this would be a good time to
get in a little practice. A
male clerk helped me select
them and when I told him, they
were on the conservative side.
he laughed and said that
a tie is to a man what a hat
is to a woman - 'a new lease
on life' and when a woman
bought a hat that went with
nothing she owned - she just
went out and bought something
it did go with. Maybe you'll
have to do the same. Any

51

why this in good marked
experience. Had to see about
my wages quota — They are
going to give me 132# a
month.

Rather get on my way
home before I get to work.

A Happy New Year
sweet — Our New Year.
We get to be together
every day this coming
year —

I miss you — loads
darling
your Bill

P.S.
I love you

See to spending N.Y. Eve on our
inventory

Girl, 21, Finds Lipstick Stains, Shoots Fiance

Woman Tells Police She Attempted Suicide

Cincinnati, Sept. 30 (AP)—A pretty 21-year-old brunet was charged with shooting with intent to kill after she admitted in a statement, Detective Chief Clem Merz said, that she shot and wounded her fiance today when she found lipstick smears on his face and shirt.

The girl, Louise Sharpe, former War Assets Administration office worker, was released on $2,000 bond furnished by her family.

The gun victim, Paul J. Streicher, 33, a druggist, was reported in serious condition at General Hospital.

Wounded Three Times

He was shot twice in the chest and once in the back, Merz said. The shooting occurred in Streicher's apartment.

Police first learned of the shooting, the detective chief reported, when Streicher telephoned headquarters and mumbled:

"My girl shot me and I'm bleeding terribly. Get me to a hospital

"Life has a way of beating us down,
perhaps because we don't see it coldly
enough to be clear about it when we
are young. Man's life is divided into
two parts: his work and his private
life. He may succeed at one, fail at
the other. And it is only when he is
old, and the time for decision is over,
that he may realize he did not need to
neglect one for the other."

I'm going to send one of these
to Leo so don't show him this.

"I wanted to die. Someone
knocked on my door and I turned
off the gas. It was the police who

About Anne

Anne Marie Standish was born in Buffalo, NY, in 1919 and died in 2004.

The hyphen between those two years, 1919-2004, may be more of a symbol than an element of grammar. In some ways, it is a sign of her many connections to other people's lives.

Anne was a devoted wife. Early on in her life, she worked as a secretary in the engineering department for a local General Motors/Chevrolet plant. She later supported Bill's tavern business in Savannah and upon returning to Buffalo, held a variety of administrative "Gal Friday" roles for businesses there. Anne always had a head for business and enjoyed managing the books for the family—whether it was investments or taxes.

Anne was like a second mother to me. Growing up, we'd see a lot of each other, as my parents and sister and I lived with Anne's mother and father, and Anne was a frequent visitor and caller on the phone. She was always ready to lend an ear and share an encouraging word.

In my own stash of letters is one she wrote to me on September 17, 1976, in response to my confidential letter to her about my struggles and homesickness as a freshman at Marquette University. Her message was "be patient."

>*...in your lifetime, you will always have some ups and downs as you get older and experience more of life and you will find that the 'Ups' far outweigh the 'Downs.' Too, if we didn't have some disappointments, how could we feel joy and happiness. We all find it in different experiences but just remember you must get that happiness from the right things because happiness from bad things only leads to unhappiness eventually anyway.*

>*What I'm trying to say Tom is let others do as they please. None of us can be the next person. There is only one TOM in the world and one ANNE. Just remember, don't be a fish or a sheep. Sometimes we see and hear things that don't seem right and you know are not right. It is not for us to say what is right and what is*

wrong. If you know what is right and wrong for you, you'll come out okay. It is a tough life but it is the only one we know and somehow or other it all evens itself out.

Again, just be patient. I've been through it Tom. I know what you are trying to say. Trust me. Give yourself time.

This is a time of learning for you and though it seems all is coming too fast, it will slow up at times and the eventual ball of wisdom and experiences that you will take out of this beautiful (sometimes cruel) world will be a composite of all these 'Ups & Downs' you are experiencing now....

Aunt Anne took her ball of wisdom with her when she died in 2004 but was survived by a bunch of letters on love.

About Bill

William A. Ross (WAR) was born (1917) and raised on the family farm on the mucklands of Savannah, NY, a community of about 1,800 people. True to his initials, Bill volunteered to serve our country during WWII as a master gunner, a role he was later recognized for.

Not fond of working on the land, Bill opened a billiard parlor and later a tavern and a restaurant. At age 24 he enlisted in the WNY-based 209th National Guard Regiment and, after some time, was sent to Ireland for training as a replacement soldier.

All the time he was away from Savannah, he paid $12 a month rent on each of his units, the billiard parlor, tavern and restaurant. His sister did not like being a replacement manager for her brother, so the business closed while he was away.

Bill would often say that his world seemed smaller after returning home from the war. He struggled to re-open a bar in his hometown when he got back as suppliers of candy and cigars had forged agreements with other locals. But, he persisted in business and in life. The 130 miles from Savannah to Buffalo in the late 1940s did not stop him from converting a long-distance relationship into a successful marriage and a happy life.

Bill met Anne Standish through Anne's cousin, Frank, who also served in the military. Following their marriage, Anne moved to Savannah for a few years to help him with his business—Marshland Restaurant. The couple later relocated to Buffalo where Bill worked in security for the Federal Reserve Bank for 27.5 years, retiring in 1980.

On Flag Day, June 14, 2006, Bill was recognized for his military service by the French Government, receiving "A Chevalier of the Legion of Honor"—France's highest honor awarded to people of all walks of life who glorify France with outstanding achievements.

He died in 2013.

Anne's Affirmations

It's a nice ring but the best part is the guy who comes with it.

I wouldn't want any part of you, if I can't have all of you.

Life is so darn short and it doesn't seem to be worthwhile to be unhappy over trifles.

Being in love is a wonderful thing and yet it isn't. A person's mind never seems to be at rest.

When a girl gets interested in everything her guy does, she is really sunk.

Make the most and best of every situation.

A person can have a lot of money and have nothing to show for it.

Never let a girl make a fool out of you. If she is nice, then be nice to her but always use a little common sense.

I can't see these people who want a lot out of life but do not want to work for it.

August 27, 1995

CPSIA information can be obtained
at www.ICGtesting.com
Printed in the USA
BVHW071526010521
606210BV00002B/241